Love Still Wins

The True Story of how you really can recover from an abusive relationship

SAMUEL P. HOLLOWAY III

© Copyright 2018 by Samuel P. Holloway III

All rights reserved.

No part of this book may be reproduced or transmitted in any form or by any means, electronic or mechanical, including photocopying, recording, or by any information storage and retrieval system, without permission in writing from the publisher Samuel P. Holloway III at SPH 3 Publishing, except in the case of brief quotations embodied in critical articles or reviews.

ISBN: 978-0-692-06792-5

10 9 8 7 6 5 4 3 2 1

Visit my website at

www.SamuelHolloway3.com

Acknowledgments

I want to acknowledge myself, please don't feel as if I'm being narcissistic. I'm acknowledging myself because I followed my heart and went with my gut before things turned ugly. So many of us stay in a relationship that we know is unhealthy for us, but we remain because we love that person or feel we can change them. However, when someone shows you who they are, believe them the first time.

I'm glad I didn't have to go through too many things or become physically hurt before I walked away. This relationship taught me no matter what, "Love Still Wins" regardless of what happens if I'm in a relationship or not! I'm grateful for the experience because it was like nothing I'd experienced before. Hopefully you, the reader, will learn from my mistakes and not have to travel this road too.

THANK YOU

I'd like to give thanks for those who've helped me with this project; Shantel Floyd for her powerful poetry, Kellie Todd for her beautiful photography in "***Love Still Wins***." Jessica Godbee for creating this master piece of a cover, and Myron Schippers for editing the book as well.

And an extra special thanks to everyone who played a negative roll within this book. Your negativity and actions helped with my growth, cultivated my strength and definitely assisted in the heart of this project.

Prologue

Have you EVER found yourself at zero? I was almost there, hovering around one is low enough! At a time when I was supposed to have been at the highest in my life, considering all the things I'd overcome, I actually was at my lowest and realized I was still going through a personal hell.

My verbally, financially and very close to physically abusive relationship had me ready to leap off the edge of the very cliff I was so desperately clinging to. I still can't believe I managed to smile through it all and I believe it was because I knew within my heart, **LOVE STILL WINS!**

Table of Contents

The Beginning 1

The Twist 5

I Wasn't Perfect 15

The Move 35

Reaching Out 49

Loyalty Is Royalty 57

Love Still Wins 61

So Numb

By Shantel Floyd

So numb to feel numb from the one I love. The one I put my faith in. The one I gave my trust to, the one I gave my heart to, to the point I lost my soul.

I only ask myself, why did I sell my soul to a person who heart is so cold?

My heart was empty. But I opened it for only him to fill that void.

In the beginning, it was smiles and laughter that made me fall in love to a point my heart was filled with joy.

Slowly my smile is fading away from the hurtful things he says. But he didn't mean it. I mean he tells me that he loves me every day.

He wipes my tears away and tells me I'm the most beautiful person on earth.

Hurtful words turning to anger now making me feel way less than what I'm worth.

Yesterday, he says, "baby don't cry, please don't be sad."
Today, I'm one minute late coming in. And now, once again he's mad.

Hurtful words turn into bruises to the heart.

Still I stay like an addict fiending for that smile from the start.

Bruises to the heart are now visible to the face.

But he loves me! I tell myself while the blood tickles my tongue for a taste.

"Why me? What did I do to be treated this way?"

I forgive that question as he makes love to me and have me sing in a warm place.

Love is like an addiction, so I just want it, I just need it, so I'll just take the risk.

But love should not hurt, and love should not ever form into a fist.

Why can't I leave him? Why do I still want to be his mate?

He tells me, "the love I want is only in a fairy tale life."

But I still stay, hoping he can see the wonderful person I am.

Only to be beat into a pulp hurting to my limbs.

I lay while he beats on me until I'm unconscious. I see the light. Lord please take my life. Take me away from him.

My child "Get up! Your life is to be great before the end!"

So, I get up, body broken, heart mentally disable, but still I walk away.
This time, I put faith in myself, now I stand greater than I ever been from that day!

And from that day, I've never been "So Numb" again because in the end, Love Still Wins!

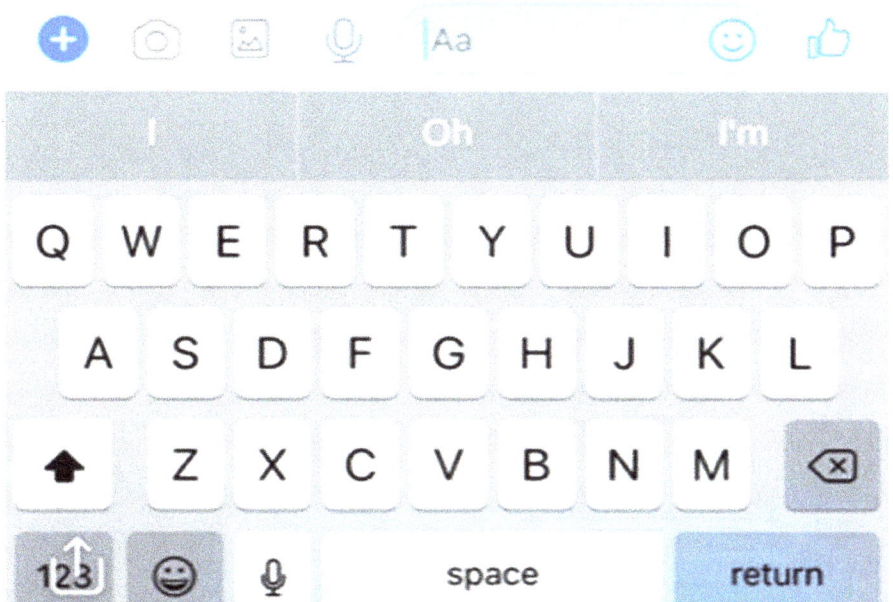

Clinton speaking to his boyfriends, best friend about Cam and me.

> Don't play my friend! He is a great guy and the gay community need more men like him! You have a track record and you should've thought about that before my friend caught feelings for you. Don't do my friend like you did Clint. He a good dude too but now my friend is with Clint and has been for a while now since you didn't treat him right. He knows you cheated on him that's why he moved on before you tried to leave him. Nobody wants pain and hurt in their heart. So it'll probably be best if you told Cam the truth now before he finds out you lied. Cam has been through hell and I can't sit back and watch someone like you do him the

Clinton's boyfriend, best friend sending me a message on Facebook.

+1 (404) 82... (706) 627-3...

iMessage
Sun, Jun 11, 12:13 AM

iMessage
Today 12:08 AM

> Why u say untag you?

This picture makes it look like I like you but I don't

> It does not bro! 😩😩😩

No I mean as a friend G

> Huh?

Man I know what you said about me trying to get wit Clinton and I ain't wit it

> I said clinton told me you were trying to get with him! I didn't say you were trying to get with him!!!
> Delivered

> Kevin can you explain this? I only told you Tim and TaQuan what clinton told me!

This picture makes it look like I like you but I don't

Discussion between my so called friends. What's interesting is they had a gathering including my ex, Clinton, along with his boyfriend, then trying to confront me afterwards.

+1 (404) 82... **(706) 627-3...**

> This picture makes it look like I like you but I don't

> It does not bro! 😩😩😩

> No I mean as a friend G

> Huh?

> Man I know what you said about me trying to get wit Clinton and I ain't wit it

> I said clinton told me you were trying to get with him! I didn't say you were trying to get with him!!!

Delivered

> I was told you were showing texts to other people that me and Clinton had...but I don't even have that nigga's number.

> And this Kevin?

+1 (404) 825-3680

> to be clear ... you said you saw text messages from Clinton not showing people ... and as anyone's friend i don't want ANYONE around me who

AT&T LTE 4:43 PM

+1 (404) 82...   (706) 627-3...

> trying to get with him! I didn't say you were trying to get with him!!!

Delivered

I was told you were showing texts to other people that me and Clinton had...but I don't even have that nigga's number.

> And this Kevin?

+1 (404) 825-3680

to be clear ... you said you saw text messages from Clinton not showing people ... and as anyone's friend i don't want ANYONE around me who clearly fucks with the notion of stealing someone's man. so i brought it up to be clear and clear the air.

(706) 627-3439

To also clear the air, Clinton stated that you said this shit too

CHAPTER 1

The Beginning

I must start out by saying that my ex-boyfriend Clinton was a great guy; he was just not the guy for me. I don't have any animosity towards him what so ever. I wish Clinton nothing but the best in his future endeavors. Everything seemed to be heading in the right direction with our relationship. I thought I'd found THE ONE, my Prince Charming, my Knight in Shining Armor.

This man was everything to me! He was kind, caring, protective, and a real family man. I loved and admired the relationship he had with his mother, they spoke all the time. The relationship with his siblings was equally appealing to me. His relationship with his father on the other hand was completely different, that relationship was reminiscent of the one I shared with my mother; nonexistent.

Clinton, his grandmother and great aunt shared a beautiful relationship too. His grandfather was another unique story, he loved his grandson, but he just didn't like the life-style that his grandson was living. I know for sure he didn't care for me and I was fine with that, I wasn't fucking him!

Clinton and I had traveled together from Florida to Delaware, New Jersey, and on to New Orleans. Everyplace we traveled, we took the four-legged babies (Brooklyn and Lacey, his dogs) with us. I always felt that we should have taken them to a kennel but Clinton was completely against that and I understood why. He'd had them for over ten plus years and they were like his children. But I still felt they hindered us from doing a lot of special things while traveling but I compromised on that situation every time.

You know, when I think back on why I fell in love with Clinton I still smile. He was the very first chocolate man I've ever loved. I loved him! I really loved him and I knew deep within my heart that he loved me! I loved him from his head to his ankles. **I'll get into them feet later** Clinton was thick, weighing in at 180 plus pounds, nice chest, big arms, deep voice, dreamy eyes and a size 13 shoe!

Side Stare

I loved him because he was everything to me, and he came with the much sought after 3 C's: Crib, Car and Career. He was a manly man. He took care of his home. He paid the deposit for us to get a new home as a birthday present for me on December 15, 2016. He wanted to see me happy and I loved it, however, he proved to be a man of many layers, much like peeling an onion, each layer came with new and challenging issues.

Clinton once told me a story about catching his ex-boyfriend in bed with another man. He worked twelve-hour shifts from 3 in the morning to 3 in the afternoon. His best friend, who rarely came around, and his mom confirmed this story, so I believed it. Clinton said his ex-treated him horribly and spoke to him in a degrading manner on a regular basis, but he was in love with him anyway. I believe that what Clinton felt about his ex and everything that he had experienced, he brought that pain with him into our relationship. With everything that I had been through with my ex-husband, Price (Paul Hill is his real name) I tried my absolute best not to bring those issues into our relationship. I had two other relationships after Paul, with #26 and #14, so I tried to only speak upon them instead of the bad with Paul. I thought I really had found the one with Clinton in my heart, mind, body and soul.

Boy oh boy, was I wrong about Clinton. What I had found was someone who wore a mask and showed his true colors as soon as his name was on a shared lease. I had found someone who was bitter, insecure, a liar, a great manipulator and someone who wouldn't even apologize when they're wrong, even if his life depended on it!

CHAPTER 2

The Twist

I was silent for four months and didn't say shit. You can't hurt anyone that doesn't care! I turned my feelings off. However, I will not allow anyone to tarnish my name or try and hurt my brand. At first, I actually felt sorry for Clinton during our break up but after some meditation and self-reflection, I realized everything he did was premeditated and planned out as if he drew a map.

Some days he would mope around the house and other days he would be so angry. Clinton would march up and down the stairs as if he was trying out for the Army. He would slam doors and cabinets. He would be angry at the dogs yelling and cursing at them as if they had done something to him. He would place his phone on speaker and call me every name in the book from a whore, slut, bitch, tramp, nasty ass nicca, a cheater, a liar and even feminine. I wasn't surprised by any of it, except being called feminine because he was feminine himself but that didn't bother me.

After being accused of cheating, starting in January, for apparently having sex with seven people (yes you read that number right 7), including my best friend Timothy, I knew I was involved with someone who was insecure. I couldn't understand it because Clinton was fine as hell in my eyes before then. Everyone who knows me knows that chocolate was not my thing. But Clinton was everything to me. I loved his chocolate ass.

On Thanksgiving, Timothy came to town and stayed with us, as usual. Clinton made sure that I told Timothy not to be in and out of the house after 11p.m. **Really?** How can you tell a grown man, with a key to my place not to come and go as he pleases?! Any who, I relayed the message because again, Clinton was my man and I didn't want nor need the drama. Timothy obliged because he loved me.

******

Our relationship changed on January 1, 2017, four days after we moved into our new home. On that day, I told Clinton that Timothy would be coming down the weekend of the 14th to Atlanta. Timothy had come down to Atlanta from North and South Carolina (he moved to North Carolina from South Carolina) every month since we've known each other. Timothy had just drove down four hours on December 27, after getting off work to help us move with no questions asked. You see none of Clinton's friends were available to help us.

My straight homie Carlos came over to help move the couches because Timothy and Clinton couldn't move them alone. Ya'll already know I don't do manual labor so once I tried to lift it and felt how heavy it was, I called Carlos. Carlos came over immediately and helped Clinton move both the couch and loveseat into the U-Haul from the third floor apartment. After Carlos left, I noticed Clinton had an attitude. I asked him if everything was okay.

Clinton stated, "Why did you call him over?"

I responded by telling him, "The couch and loveseat were heavy, I couldn't lift it and neither could the both of you, it's getting late, Carlos moved me into this apartment so why not call him?!"

Clinton was pissed! Then he had the nerve to say, "And I saw him looking at your ass too!" Timothy and I looked at each other in disbelief. I reassured Clinton that Carlos is straight and I've known him for almost five years at that point! Although Carlos is fine as hell, that was a line that I never crossed and I didn't have the slightest hint that Carlos fucked around with men. Now if he did, I would have been first in line! HELLO

After loading the rest of the big stuff, we all left and headed to the new house. Once there, Timothy helped us unload the heavy furniture. Clinton asked him if he wanted to spend the night considering it was late and he knew he had to be tired after coming from work straight here to help us move. Timothy declined giving both of us a hug, congratulating us on the new house and headed back off to North Carolina.

The next day my friend Kevin came over to the old place after work and helped us load our cars up, even his and we all went back to the new house where we unloaded everything. Once again, none of Clinton's friends came to help us. By January 1, 2017, we were settled into our 3-bedroom, 2-bathroom, 2-car garage home. It was immaculate with stainless steel appliances, hardwood floors on the first level and new carpet on the second level, along with not just one but two living rooms.

For safety concerns, Clinton had a security system installed immediately. He had four cameras outside and wanted to place five to seven cameras on the inside of the house. I told Clinton that day, if you place any cameras in this home, I won't be living in it. To me, having cameras on the inside seemed a bit extreme considering that cameras were placed at every entrance of the home including the camera in the garage, which was directly focused on my car! **Side Stare**

On the 13th of every month Clinton and I celebrated our anniversary in recognition of the day we had met on July 13, 2015. Clinton felt that Timothy should not come that weekend because it was our anniversary and he had planned something special for us. Clinton said, "This isn't just your home, you don't stay alone and you didn't even ask me if Timothy could come anyway!"

"*Ask* you?" I said! Now I was pissed at the fact that I had to ask if my best friend could come down. It wasn't like Timothy could have messed up our weekend considering what Clinton had planned anyway.

We had a big house and Timothy could have been in a separate room and used a separate bathroom. Hell, when Timothy did come down, we would spend a day together and Timothy would spend the rest of his time with family, friends and whatever else he was doing. Clinton just didn't want Timothy around I would find out why later. I decided to call Timothy and tell him that he couldn't stay with us that weekend and told him why and that it wasn't my decision.

Timothy was shocked because Clinton had no problem with him driving down from North Carolina, after he'd just got off work to help us move and then make a midnight drive back to North Carolina! I was hurt and pissed but I didn't want any conflict within my relationship, so once again, I compromised. During the weekend of our anniversary of January 13, we didn't do shit but cook on Saturday, have dinner at home and went to the Drive Inn! **Pissed Off Look**

******

Clinton had been coming home early from work some nights at this point. He would leave around 2:20am and usually return by 4pm if traffic wasn't bad. The last week of January he had start coming home early. One day in particular, he called and said, "I will be home early because they (the job) don't have any work for us." He worked for a solar company here in Atlanta.

That day right after he called, I heard the garage door opening. Clinton's job was a good 30 minutes away but he was home right after he called! On February 2, Clinton went to work and was informed that everyone was being laid off! Laid off with no unemployment benefits because Clinton said he owed unemployment from when he was laid off before. On top of that he felt he was too good to go and apply for food stamps. Shit, my ass went and applied for food stamps and only received $16! I wasn't too good!

Time had gone by since the debacle with Timothy, it was February 17th. My friends and I had planned that we would all meet here in Atlanta everyone lived in another state, except for Kevin. We usually meet up once a year and this time we would be meeting here in Atlanta, therefore everyone would be staying with us, after all we had enough room. ***I asked Clinton well ahead of time!***

I thought this was going to be a weekend to remember considering all my friends would be here. I had no other gay friends in Atlanta other than Kevin and I truly missed everyone. I needed my friends in my life because I had no family here and they were truly my family without a shadow of a doubt.

TaQuan and David flew in first from New Jersey on Friday morning February 17th. Clinton was laid off from his job at that point and greeted them at the house because I didn't get out of class until later that afternoon. Kevin came over after getting off work and he and I went to pick up George from the airport. My Bestie Timothy arrived around 8ish driving in from North Carolina. Timothy wasn't coming at first but we all begged him to, it wouldn't have been a party without my Bestie! Moe didn't arrive from Houston until later that night.

Once we were all together it was everything, I was smiling ear to ear! I had all my friends and my man under one roof in our new home and we were hosting so it was nothing less than great! Unfortunately, this was going to be a weekend I was going to remember for the rest of my life, and not for a good reason either.

Friday, after everyone arrived, we all sat around talked, laughed and read each other. That was just how our group was. Whatever we said behind another's back, we would say it to their face, for the most of us. We all ordered American Deli and Sharon came over before we went out to the club. Dexter and his boyfriend Elliot met us at our house before we went to the club to pre-game.

Immediately, Clinton caught an attitude because I didn't ask him if they could come over! Whatever, I ignored his nonsense because my friends were here. When we arrived at the club, I realized I had left my driver's license in my car. Being that Clinton drove, I didn't check to see if I had had my ID.

Clinton and I ended up turning right back around and making that 40-minute drive back home to get my ID and back to the club just in time for TaQuan and David to get into it at Bulldogs. TaQuan and David were dealing with some issues that should have remained in their home in New Jersey. Regardless of what they were going through, that situation was not for the club and definitely not in front of us.

I pulled TaQuan away from David as they were arguing and Clinton pulled David away. No more than 15 minutes had passed and before I knew it Clinton and I were getting into it right after because he was angry that Paul had been calling my phone and I had spoken to Paul's ex-boyfriend's best friend. **Really** Right after that, I was over it and ready to go. I told Clinton, "This is not the time nor the place to do some dumb shit like that!"

We all left and headed back to our place. When we got there, everyone went into the house except Clinton and David. At this point, they had become best friends after this being just their second-time meeting. David was telling Clinton everything that had gone on within he and TaQuan's relationship and Clinton was an ear for him.

Saturday morning, David, Moe and myself went grocery shopping for breakfast. I spoke to David about TaQuan and gave examples of Clinton and myself relationship and how no relationship is perfect but you must talk about things as they arise instead of waiting and letting that anger build up. Later that evening we ordered chicken from JJ Fish & Chicken. Vernetta, Cherie, her sister, Miyasha and everyone else was there. We played spades, drank and danced. Then Clinton and TaQuan got into it.

Taquan and Clinton were in the kitchen and I walked in on their conversation. They were speaking about "apologizing when someone is wrong in a relationship."

I cut in the conversation and said, "Clinton has never, ever, apologized to me and most of the time he's in the wrong."

Clinton replied, "I shouldn't have to apologize for anything in my house, and if I'm wrong, I'll buy a bottle of alcohol, cook a big dinner and we will have sex!"

TaQuan started tapping Clinton on his chess with his pointer finger and said, "Clinton, that's not right, sometimes you have to apologize!"

Clinton blew up and started yelling, telling TaQuan, "Don't touch me and don't tell me what I need to say in my own damn house!"

TaQuan apologized and said he was just playing and didn't know that Clinton was offended and apologized again!

Clinton was still offended and David came to Clinton's rescue. I went upstairs into the master bedroom bathroom and closed the door. I was pissed, shocked and couldn't believe how Clinton had just reacted. Clinton then burst into the bathroom telling me I was wrong for not sticking up for him. I told Clinton, "You're single! Do whatever the fuck you want to do because I don't give a fuck anymore!"

That day, I fell out of love with the man I once was in love with. How could you react like that to my friend?!

Sunday morning there was a cloud looming over our home. Clinton had slept downstairs on the couch, TaQuan wasn't speaking to David and all my friends had witnessed something that they were not supposed to see. I don't even remember everyone leaving that night.

Early Sunday morning Moe and George left because of everything that had happened. Moe ended up sitting at the airport until later that evening. We had planned on cooking a big dinner that day but no one was in the mood to cook. However, we were hungry so TaQuan, Timothy and I went to pick up Miyasha and headed to the grocery store. TaQuan and I cooked dinner but everything TaQuan cooked was nasty as hell. LOL **Shade**

Timothy left later that evening. The rest of the night seemed awkward as David, TaQuan, Kevin and myself watched Real Housewives of Atlanta and some other bullshit on TV that I can't even remember. Clinton was in and out of the house, slamming the door, making the alarm go off and marching up and down the stairs. I was totally embarrassed by his childish actions.

Early Monday morning TaQuan left at 2 a.m. and took the rental car with him. He apologized to me and asked me to apologize to Clinton because he didn't mean any harm and didn't try to disrespect our home or relationship. I told him there was no apology needed because Clinton went overboard, he knew he was wrong by never apologizing and to hear it from someone else only pissed him off!

Everyone left because they didn't feel comfortable! David was the last to leave and Clinton took him to the airport because I wasn't going to. David confronted me in my home and told me that I shouldn't have been going to TaQuan for any advice. David told me I should have come to him! *Oh really?* I thought! David had only known Clinton that weekend, that was their second-time meeting and David told Clinton everything about their relationship and even lied on me! Fuck Outta Here!!!!!

After everyone left, Clinton cut up all the pictures of us and our friends throughout the entire house leaving our walls bare; with just paintings and pictures that were mine. I told Clinton that if we're going to get back together, he had to apologize to all my friends and we needed to go to counseling. Clinton said he would apologize when he got ready and that we would go to counseling because he wanted our relationship to work because he was in love with me.

However, Clinton never reached out to anyone! He never apologized to anyone! All my friends including TaQuan ended up reaching out to him and apologizing. Clinton did send Timothy a long text message to reply to later in the week but there was no apology included. **Blank Stare** We ended up getting back together because I loved him but I knew in my heart that men may come and go, but best friends are forever.

CHAPTER 3

I Wasn't Perfect

My inappropriate conversations were not inappropriate, but Clinton thought they were. I had two people reach out to me and Clinton took those conversations the wrong way without asking me the content of them. Everything you read isn't what it is if you don't read it, in its entirety! It was at this point that porn became my best friend. I didn't want him to touch me at all! I had no sexual feelings for Clinton what-so-ever.

A guy on Facebook named Boopie hit me up on messenger. Boopie and I had sex three years ago before I knew Clinton. Boopie knew I was in a relationship because my Facebook page was full of pictures of Clinton and me. However, he didn't care and still proceeded to inbox me and say, "Can I have some of that good pussy?" Unfortunately, I replied a couple of days later.

My response was cute and to the point. My first reply back was, "Nicca I know you see I'm in a whole relationship! And even if I wasn't, I still wouldn't fuck you again because the dick wasn't even worth it!"

Boopie was still trying to get on but I wasn't going. While I was at school, Clinton got my laptop and hacked into my messenger and read the message from Boopie and I'm quite sure all the other messages in my inbox too. I didn't care because I didn't have anything to hide. My homegirl and school sista, Diane called my phone and asked did I have my laptop. I told her no and it was at home. Diane told me I might need to leave school and head home because Clinton was posting screen shots from my laptop saying, "I was cheating."

Instead of looking for a damn job, this nicca was going through my shit looking for something that couldn't be found. But the saying is true, "If you go looking for something you will find it!" Before I arrived home, I called the police because I only had two months before I would be graduating with my Bachelors degree and I didn't need the extra drama from an insecure motherfucker who was angry about his life. At this point, all my friends were still "Team Clinton" but I wasn't! I just wanted to be alone because I didn't feel we had anything left for a relationship and I was not in the business of changing someone who didn't want to change.

The second message was from James. I met James at a gay house party along with Kevin. Clinton didn't go with me; we were not speaking after getting into it about Boopie. At the party there were a bunch of feminine men and James was the only masculine man there. He was alone against the wall with a drink in his hand. I had my drink and I kept looking at him and once our eyes connected, he called me over.

I walked over, introduced myself and he introduced himself. We went through the where you from, (he was from Atlanta) what's your sign, (He is a Leo) I told him I don't get along well with Leo's except my friends that are Leo's. We laughed hard. Then the question came about, "Were we single or in a relationship?" We realized we were both in relationships with issues from someone being insecure. We laughed and started talking about what we did as far as business. James was a promoter and offered to promote my book. We talked for most of the night before Kevin and I headed out.

James and I connected on Facebook during our conversation. He was headed to an after party and Kevin and I were headed to Krystal's to get a bite to eat. James asked me to hit him up when I got home, we'd been drinking and by now it was pouring down raining so it was time to head home. After stopping at Krystal's, I left Kevin and headed home. It was almost 4am. When I got home, I called Kevin and told him I made it, then I received a message from James on messenger.

James said, "I enjoyed you."

I replied, "I enjoyed you too."

He then "Liked" my fan page for my book *Eyes Without A Face* and sent his phone number. I called, and we chatted a minute and he asked to make sure he received a copy of my book. After that we hung up. Clinton read that message and blew up! He assumed that when we said we "enjoyed each other" that meant we fucked!

I told Clinton to call Kevin and ask him if I left with James and he did, and Kevin told him no, that was impossible because I was with him the entire time. Clinton said I could have left the house and did. It just didn't make any sense to me. I called James and told him what transpired because of his message and James told me, "It would have been nice to promote your book but I can't do the insecure boyfriend thing because I have one myself so I'll pass on that bro!" I was pissed off but I totally understood. I would have done the same thing myself.

March, Clinton had no job, no car, and I felt like he was a cokehead. We had a huge argument somewhere in the beginning of

March and I left the house, Clinton stayed behind and got drunk. That night when I returned home, Clinton was not there. Early the next morning I was looking at the camera monitor and noticed a white car pulling into the driveway. After a while, Clinton emerged from the passenger side of the car and came into the house through the garage like usual. I was pissed and hurt because I felt like he stayed out and cheated to get back at me thinking I cheated.

I called Kevin because he was the only one who was not at work at the time. I was crying because my feelings were hurt. I told Kevin how Clinton just came home from yesterday and was dropped off by someone. Although I couldn't see who dropped him off, he left right back out walking up the street. Kevin told me I needed to call Clinton. He was so persistent that I hung up and called Clinton.

Clinton answered the phone and I asked him where had he been? Clinton responded and said, "I was in a car accident after you left yesterday. I dropped my phone on the floor while driving, went to pick it up and swerved to not hit the car in front of me and hit the curb and tore my car up! I spent most of the night in the hospital and Todd came and got me. I stayed with him for the night. Todd just dropped me off at the house, but I left to go meet my homegirl."

I was in tears because I really loved him. My emotions were everywhere. I asked, "Why didn't you call me?"

Clinton said, "Because you were angry and I didn't think you would answer!"

I said, "Come on now, I don't give a fuck how angry I am at you, if you're hurt, I need to know!

Clinton said, "I called Kevin!"

In my mind, I was thinking, *Are you fucking Kevin?!* But the red flag went up immediately because Kevin didn't tell me, and it also let me know they had a closer relationship than I thought. I started thinking, *This is exactly how Kevin lost his boyfriend to his best friend.*

Clinton's car was in the shop for some time until I realized he wasn't getting it back. His grandparents sent him some money to pay his deductible but he never got the car back. The only thing I could think was the car was repossessed. He was behind on payments and blamed me because he paid the security deposit for us to move into our new home. Go figure!

Clinton posted on Facebook that I was broke and just using him. He said I was only bringing in $1,500 a month, hadn't had a job in seven years and I was a cheater." Really nicca! That's just like a bitter person to tell half the story and not even the whole truth at that. Yes, I hadn't had a job in 7 years. I was bringing in enough to cover bills, plus my book sale revenue. You can't use no one that doesn't have shit and I was far from a cheater!

When I met Clinton, I had about $3,000 in the bank, a couple of credit cards with no balances and I was traveling with Timothy any time I wanted to with no questions asked. I knew what I could do and what I couldn't do because I wasn't living beyond my means or trying to impress people that didn't have shit! I couldn't work because I suffer from PTSD after the carjacking, robbery and nearly being killed after being set up by my ex-husband. However, I was surviving long before I met Clinton and doing it without struggling or asking anyone for anything and my bills were always paid on time!

But by March, I was completely broke! I didn't have a dime in the bank, my credit cards were maxed out, I had bills overdue and we barley even had food at times. How in the hell is that possible when you have two people in a relationship? You should never get that low to where you're wondering how you're going to eat! That motherfucker was all about himself! That's it, that's all!

After telling Clinton I spent my savings to save his financial ass, this bastard said I should have gotten a part time job or something, then I wouldn't be broke! "Oh, really mother fucker?!" I said. "How about you're the one with no income, while my money is paying all the bills in this bitch, including your cell phone bill! You're the one that needs a job, not me!"

Once I arrived home, the police were pulling up as well. When I pulled into the driveway and opened the garage door, I noticed immediately how the blinds in the living room window had one blind open as if Clinton was standing there looking out. I didn't know if he was home because he didn't have a car.

The police officers parked on the street and I walked to meet them in the driveway. There was a black officer and a white officer. They asked me what happened and I told them. They asked if Clinton was in the house and I told them I didn't know. They walked in the house with me and I called out to Clinton. He didn't answer and I checked the home and informed the officers he was not there as they waited in the living room.

The white officer walked back to the patrol car and the black officer took notes from our conversation on what had happened. The black police officers name was Cam! He gave me a case number and then gave me his phone number and told me to call if I needed him or just wanted to talk.

When Clinton came back home, the police officers had just left. I believe he was somewhere watching because he came right after they pulled off. I was putting my laptop in my backpack downstairs as he walked through the garage door. Clinton said, "You can take your laptop with you but I didn't use that to catch you cheating. I used the mainframe because all the electronics are hooked up to it!"

I'd had the internet and cable turned off because he wasn't helping with the bills. So, how in the hell could he use the mainframe?! I just ignored his insecure ass and went back to school. He was not about to fuck up my education and I was close to graduating. I realized that we were arguing now on a regular basis and every morning that I had to take an exam became unbearable. I would stay up all night to study for an exam and as soon as I would get ready to leave, this nicca would try and argue. I was good for walking out the door and saying, "Okay!" Silence will kill a motherfucker more than words!

By March 16, maybe a few days later, not even a week, Clinton's mother sent me a text message. One night I was studying for an exam and watching *The Golden Girls* upstairs in the bedroom with the door closed. Clinton busted in the bedroom and started cursing me out. He was angry that I had been ignoring him and wanted to know if I was cheating. I really didn't have anything to say. I had just written him a letter while I was trying to study but I needed to get out what I had to say.

I ended up sending the letter out after our conversation, only after I saw him on the camera in the garage cocking his gun and coming into the house. It scared me so instead of calling the police, I sent the letter out to my sister, Timothy, TaQuan, Diane, his sister and his mother. I was scared and I titled the email "A letter just in case from Samuel about Clinton."

THE LETTER
March 15, 2017

Clinton,

    I'm sure you know at this point our relationship is over and irreconcilable at this point. The main reason for this split is that seven weeks before I graduate that you would pull all kinds of childish stunts and verbally abuse me during this time. From posting all over social media that I cheated on you to verbal and physical threats, is totally unacceptable and uncalled for.

    I'm supposed to be spending this time with my head deep in my work but instead I'm receiving screenshots and calls from friends, family and other concerned people because your insecurity and posts on social media have them worried about my safety. I am attaching the screenshot from James Ebony being that you are accusing me of having sex with him only because I'm not having sex with you. In fact, the day you accused me of cheating, I was in the house all day doing homework—you were the one not home all day. It's a shame that you would think that but generally when someone is doing wrong, they think someone else is doing wrong. My focus is my future, my education, my goals, my dreams and nothing, including you, will stop me from achieving them.

    Furthermore, why would you even want to be with someone who is done you wrong, is always wrong and doesn't love you? I've never been with anyone who slams doors around the house every time they're upset or run to Facebook to tell the world their relationship issues. That does not attract my attention and it only pushes me further away.

I can't believe I actually have to write a letter to talk to you. Wait a minute, yes I can, only because we can never have a conversation without you raising your voice or cursing at me. You listen to respond rather than listening to understand. Every conversation is not a debate to prove who's right.

Unfortunately, our time has come to an end. The road was long and I want no part of it any longer. You have some deep rooted issues that you need professional counseling to understand. You have many issues that you've never dealt with and you lied and jumped straight into this relationship without getting over your last relationship. I done that too and had similar issues before.

When you said loudly that you should "Beat my ass to make me love you the way you want me too" "I must like getting my ass whopped because that's all I dated was nicca's that whopped my ass" and "People get killed in relationships for playing with other people's heart" you totally lost me and what little respect I had left for you. All those statements didn't make me angry; it hurt my heart, made me deeply disappointed in you and scared me. I didn't reply because I didn't want to provoke you to hit me because you've seemed unstable these last couple of weeks. However, it let me know for sure that I needed to end this abusive verbal relationship.

You called me "A money hungry Bitch" yet you haven't paid any utilities since January other than your half of the rent which you were short $200.00 in February and $325.00 on the Xfinity bill. Just to ensure that you are aware of what a "money hungry bitch" is? That's someone that's out to get your money. Within this ENTIRE relationship, you have NEVER placed ANY money in my hand for ME! Now sometimes we tend to forget some things so I may need to remind you about how money has come to you from me which has still never been paid back....And first I'm going to acknowledge that you did pay for the security deposit here of $1000 and you also paid for haircuts every now and then, we both have. But I've also helped you well:

Feb, 2016- $500 car payment
Nov 5, 2016- $104 rental car
Nov 7, 2016- $1,515 rental car
Jan 27, 2017- $200 Allstate
Feb 13, 2017- $192 Geico
Feb 13, 2017- $166.45 cell phone

So when you called me a "money hungry bitch" I was confused and flabbergasted. I helped you because I loved you and that's what you are supposed to do when your mate doesn't have it. However, when you got paid from a 2 day check and spent your money on "WEED" that is a serious problem. You could have put food in the house but instead you brought a meal—for that night only. The entire month of February you had no income and your grandmother sent you money to pay your part of the rent. But you still had weed and alcohol every single day. How is that even possible? I know the weed man is not giving you "free" weed! Either you got weed on credit or you did something to get it. I honestly don't care but that lets me know that your priorities are not in place. You stated "I don't see you getting a part time job and you only bring in $1,600 plus your school check and book sales!" I've lived off that $1,600, plus my school check and book sales and I have NEVER been behind on ANY bill! NEVER! Why would I get a part time job when I'm in school about to graduate and I'm not the one who's struggling! Anybody that is in your position would have gotten a part time job, did Uber or even applied for some type of assistance. But you did nothing except fill out more job applications and made up copies for your cleaning service. I wish you nothing but the best but you need something NOW and not later. I don't understand your priorities and I can't make you either.

 I've learned when people are checking up on you or don't believe you, generally they're doing something that they are not supposed to be doing and it's simply a guilty reaction to do so. I guess I had taken too long to come home from the gym last Thursday because you posted under Kevin's FB post of him out playing pool and stated "I see you took a break from the gym to play pool." He responded and told you that was after the pool. I generally return home between 10-10:15 from the gym but we started late that day because he had to work over. After we left the gym, I talked to your sister the ENTIRE way home! I stopped at the gas station, Papa Johns (but they were closed) then to the grocery store and picked up a pizza and salad food. But that entire situation brings back the statement of how I told you that you are possessive. If you felt something, you could have just called my phone rather than reaching posting on Kevin's Facebook page to try to catch me in a lie.

Further, you can't take accountability or responsibility for anything that you do wrong. It goes back to the statement you made towards TaQuan when you cursed him out for tapping you on your chest to let you know that when a person is wrong, you have to apologize for your actions. As a man we all have egos and pride but when you are in a relationship, sometimes those things have to be checked at the door. I do it all the time! But as you stated "I don't have to apologize if I'm wrong, I will just go buy a bottle of alcohol and cook a big dinner and that is my apology!" That is far from an apology and it's actually a slap in the face. But I put up with that for a long time. I pray when you enter your new relationship because more than likely you will soon because you can't be alone, that you use this letter as a take away and learn from your mistakes. I surely learned from mine with you.

This was the best relationship that I had ever had AT FIRST! But now, this is the second worse relationship and I know going forward I will ask many questions before getting in anything new. You scare me! Your words scare me! I had to let my family members and friends know because of your statements that if anything happened to me, Clinton did it or he had me set up! It's sad I am scared and fear for my life in a home that I share with you.

I definitely feel you have some unresolved issues with your mother for throwing you out when you were younger, your father and the feeling of abandonment and being used and your grandparents, I can't pin point it but you are definitely dealing with the trauma of some or all of those experiences in your life—I know because I dealt with them myself. All those issues in addition to your ex or ex's spewed into this relationship. By you not having counseling or dealing with these significant issues, you can't see the underlying problem. You can't continue to play victim with every situation.

Your mom told me when I first met her that you need attention. Unfortunately I can't give you all the attention that you need. I can only give you what I have. I've learned that you must first love yourself before trying to love someone else. I had to learn to love myself all over again. I didn't grow up with love and didn't receive love in my first relationship. My love came with my counseling. I may not show you that I love you the way you want me to but that does not mean that I don't love you. We all give love in many different ways.

Now our friend's situation is a whole different issue. You could care less if you're around your friends. You lied to your friends about going out or just to have drinks on three separate occasions that I know for a fact because I saw the text messages in your phone. I didn't go through your phone although we both had each other codes and passwords. Will texted you one night to go out but you were sleep. I read the previous text messages and you had told him that I was sick one time and I had the flu the other. That made me go to Todd's messages and you did the same with him and used me as an excuse. That's not right because you kill your relationships with your friends when you get into a relationship. You can't be around your mate 24/7! But now your entire pattern has changed and you go hang out with friends or whatever you do more than ever. I wish you would have done that while we were together but you always said you didn't have the money to hang out or even money for gas. What happened because you still don't have the money?!

You knew I only had 5 straight friends and 1 gay friend that live here in Atlanta. All my other gay friends live out of state. I lost 2 straight friends because I didn't want to hang out anymore because you had to be everywhere that I go or you would have an attitude. That's sad bro! My friends barely even come around. I tried to integrate our circles together but you made every excuse for that not to happen. My friends have been there for me through thick and thin—even when my life was in danger. They are my family here and I feel like you're trying to take that away because you want me all to yourself. And I'm sorry that you don't have that same type of relationship with your friends but that isn't right at all.

In closing, we need to start separating things; I want all the utilities out of my name. I have never had to pay a deposit for Georgia Power in all the 6 years I've been living here in Atlanta. You can care less about your credit but I'm not you, I cherish mine. You can set up the utilities in your name and I will pay my balances off being that I have been paying them since January with no help.

It' truly unfortunate that things have come to this because I did love you Clinton, with all my heart. However, you are a difficult person to love because of your controlling nature, insecurity and anger issues. Unlike you, I will not take to social media to trash you as you are doing me, because that ain't my style and as I said earlier, that makes you look bad.

I wish you the very best and I hope that our separation can orderly and respectful. If you feel that's not possible, please let me know and I will request a police escort while we gather our things or make other arrangements.

Relationships are like butterflies; if you hold it too tight, you will crush it. If you hold it too loose, you'll let it go forever.

Signed by,

Someone who is truly scared and afraid of living in this house with you.

Samuel P. Holloway III 3/15/2017

******

Apparently, instead of his mother texting or calling asking me questions about the letter or what had been going on between Clinton and I, she sent me a couple of long ass text messages cursing me out and disrespecting me. I was in class and had to step out after reading a couple of them. I let Diane read them before I stepped out so she could see how Clinton's mother was talking me. My first instinct was to step out the classroom, call her and curse her ass straight the fuck out!

But I was raised to respect my elders, nor would I have wanted anyone to disrespect my own mother. Instead, I took the high road and asked her why she felt like she could call me bitches, sluts, whores, a liar, basically everything her son called me. She told me again after reading her text messages that her son would never lie to her! I was just spoiled and trying to use her son and he took me out of a bad apartment and placed me into a lovely home and I had the nerve to be unappreciative. She stated that he paid his bills on time because she along with her mother had been sending him money, so I was lying! He needs to buy weed to deal with you! She went on to say that being that my mother didn't love me, that was why my life was a complete and total mess!

BITCHHHHHHHH! (I didn't say that but I paused before I read her ass in a very polite and respectable way!)

I told Clinton's mother, "First of all, your son's bills are not paid! I paid his cell phone bill! I paid the portion of the utility bills until I couldn't pay them any longer and they are in my name! Your son is a cokehead! There is no way on GOD's green earth that a fool would spend his last dollar on weed, instead of buying food to eat! And lastly, because I must get back to class, if my life is a mess because my mother doesn't love me, then your life is really fucked up! You put your son out at 16 because he's gay, your parents raised him since then, and you and your mother don't even speak. Now check that!" Then I hung up. I sent her copies of all the utilities showing her the past due amounts since she thought I was lying.

Fuck her and the boat she road in on. However, I did text her as soon as I got out of class and apologized if I disrespected her because that wasn't my intent but she was talking to me like I was her child, and I am not!

During this time, I had been going to the gym with Kevin three nights a week, and sometimes on Saturday when he wasn't drunk from the previous day. We would meet soon as he got off work around 8:30ish pm. We would work out for 1 hour and 15 minutes. I felt like we bonded during our workout sessions. We talked a lot about our relationships.

Some days his Jack'd would be going off while we would be working out. I wanted to know who in the gym with us was gay, so I would ask to see his phone to look. I never saw anyone on his phone in the gym with us but there sure was some eye candy every time we went to the gym. I wasn't blind so I could still look.

Clinton and I hadn't broken up; we just had some major issues that were unresolved.

Looking at the fine ass men would make me work out extra hard! They were all cut up and they were truly my motivation! Other days Kevin would be on Tumbler. Tumbler from his phone was nothing but mini porn scenes so I downloaded it to my phone. It wasn't like I was trying to hook up with anyone, but this was just another porn site to me. Hell, porn was my best friend and Clinton and I were not really having sex like that. I just wasn't into him.

One night after leaving the gym I decided to call Clinton's sister. I had cancelled our tickets to Las Vegas to his sister's wedding. I wasn't about to pay for that shit with everything that was going on and how his mother had disrespected me and he didn't have shit to say about it. I told his sister how Clinton said in February his mother was real sick and he was dealing with a lot and that was part of the reason that we had gotten into then because I was unsupportive when she went into the hospital. Clinton said his mother was on a ventilator and she may die!

His sister started laughing. She said that was not true! Her mother was okay and had gotten better and was out of the hospital and out with friends now! WOW! SMDH! I went on to tell her how insecure her brother is and how he constantly checks for me to see where I am without trying to make it look like he was. She said she couldn't see that because that wasn't her brother. I hung up from her about an hour later because it was going on 11pm and I knew Clinton would be looking out the window wondering where I was.

*****

March 28th weekend was Clinton's sister's wedding in Las Vegas. I didn't attend and wasn't planning on it after his mother called telling me off. I didn't want to be in her presence at all. I also cancelled our tickets so Clinton had to find another way to get there. His family came together and bought him a last-minute ticket to Vegas so he could see his sister walk down the aisle.

I was surprised because this insecure motherfucker asked me what was I going to do for the weekend. I said, "LIVE!" TaQaun was coming in town to help me with my research paper that was required for graduation. I had never done a research paper before and I was not doing it right because my professor kept putting slash marks on the starting process of writing a research paper that we had to turn in.

I took Clinton to the airport early that morning. I came back home and got my life while watching porn before TaQuan arrived. I could have cheated if I wanted too. I could have called Boopie, I could have downloaded Jack'd, hell I could just have walked downtown. I live in Atlanta and the gays are everywhere!

TaQuan came straight over from the airport to my place and we worked on my research paper all Friday evening before he left. TaQuan was a guru and my research paper was about "Socio-Economic Issues Within the African American Community." I was sure to receive an A because I worked my ass off and I have the best helping me with it.

Right before we were done with my paper, TaQuan wanted to show me a DVD he had done for his job about an upcoming event they were having. As he moved things around under the TV trying to see where the remote was for the DVD player, we discovered the spy camera under the TV along with a microphone! WHAT THE FUCK?!!!!

This nicca was watching us! I was totally blown away because he was really watching me and only GOD knows how long it had been there! We didn't even watch the DVD and went back to the paper before I lost focus. Of course, we unhooked everything and I bullshit you not, Clinton called about ten minutes later! He and his family were out to eat. He asked what I was doing and I said finishing my research paper. He then asked about the dogs, since I was watching them.

I asked about his family, and the wedding and he said everyone was sitting right next to him. Everyone spoke except his hateful ass, picking a side mother! Go figure! We hung up and I went back to my paper.

By the time we were finished with my paper, Kevin had arrived. We pre-gamed and headed to Mixx nightclub. When I say I was celebrating, I was celebrating! I had to complete my research paper to graduate and I was ready to turn up! By the end of the night, I was drunk. We were just about to leave heading out the door passing the dance floor when this redbone grabbed me. We started dancing and before I knew it, our arms were wrapped around each other and we were looking at one another in the face.

Kevin kept trying to pull me away but I was in a zone. He kept saying, "If Clinton finds out you're dancing with someone, he's going to kill you! You do remember you have a boyfriend?" I didn't give a fuck. I was just dancing. It wasn't like I was about to fuck this boy, although I honestly wanted to! When the Rhianna song "Rehab" went off, we all headed out. Reggie, the redbone I was dancing with, walked out with us and gave me his number. Shit, I wish I would have used it now! **Laughing Hard As Hell**

As soon as we pulled off in TaQuan's rental car, Kevin thought he had seen his ex-boyfriend's current boyfriend who was his best friend. Confusing, I know. But Kevin's best friend ended up with Kevin's ex-boyfriend. I'll get into that story later. Kevin jumped out of the moving car trying to go fight this boy knowing that he can't fight!

So being a good friend, once the car was stopped, I jumped out to go chase Kevin down to make sure he didn't get beat up trying to act tuff. Kevin didn't see his ex-best friend! We headed back to my place and TaQuan spent the night but Kevin was in his feelings about his ex and said he was going home. Clinton ended up calling my phone a little after 5 a.m. and asked how did I enjoy the club?

Dumbfounded, I asked how did he know I had gone to the club? Clinton said, "I know everyone in Atlanta, I have eyes on you at all times, you never know who be in the same place as you!" He went on to say his friend Todd had seen me in the club. I said, "And Todd ass couldn't speak?" Then Clinton said, "How you go be drunk trying to help Kevin fight?" I was really fucked up by that question! How the fuck did he know about that?

Clinton then said Kevin had just called him and told him about what went on! I said, "Kevin called you at 5am in the fucking morning!?" Of course, soon as I hung up, I called Kevin and told him "don't be fucking calling my man telling him shit about me, let alone don't be fucking calling him at that time of the night!" Kevin said, "Well ya'll were sleep and I needed someone to talk too!" I hung up on his shady ass! Hell, he probably told Clinton about me dancing with the boy too! At that point, I started questioning Kevin's loyalty. I believe he was still upset that I had a little thing with his nephew a while ago.

CHAPTER 4

The Move

I think Clinton returned from Vegas on April 2nd, that Tuesday. I'm not even sure because at that point I really didn't care. But I still was trying to make it work. I had prepared a dinner; spaghetti, garlic bread and string beans. I would say I cleaned the house but I always kept a clean house. I did however, leave the spy camera along with the microphone on top of the DVD player so when he walked through the garage door, that would be the very first thing he saw other than the babies.

Clinton called when he arrived at the airport. He called and said to pick him up at the train station instead of the airport so I didn't have to drive that far out. I was cool with that because I didn't want to leave the house period. I had already been drinking and I was a little buzzed. At this point in our relationship, I was drinking heavily. Let me quit lying, I was got damn alcoholic! I would get so drunk, I wouldn't even remember the night before. That's exactly how I liked it after a while. I just wanted to forget everything!

Soon as Clinton walked through the door and saw his equipment sitting out, he lost it. He started yelling, "I didn't have that set up to watch you! I had that set up to watch the dogs!"

I was calm, cool and collective and replied, "You had that fucking camera positioned straight on the fucking couch! Who the fuck you think you fooling!"

He couldn't take my response and started saying how he loved me, he wanted to come home and just chill and tell me about his trip, the wedding and have sex!

Whatever! I was drunk by that time. Every time he opened his mouth, I took a shot. I had brought a bottle of Amsterdam Vodka and by the time he was done talking, the bottle was gone! I went upstairs into the master bathroom, jacked off and went to sleep! I don't remember if he said anything to me after I walked up the stairs bumping into the wall. Unfortunately, I do remember falling into the tub after I was done stroking my dick!

That morning, Clinton woke me up by taking off my clothes. I was saying no, but I really meant yes! Before I knew it, he had my legs spread and was inside of me. He was very aggressive and telling me, "Take this dick!" I was loving it honestly. However, he came within ten minutes. I went into the bathroom, got cleaned up and thought about how we just had sex. Clinton had gone back downstairs and was lying on the couch. He had been sleeping on the couch since the saga with his momma.

I asked him, "Come fuck me again how you just did!" He came back upstairs and we did a repeat. It was everything! Our sex life was once freaky and exciting. We would have sex in the window in the living room watching the cars drive by, in front of mirrors, and walking around the house. I think all that went away after his mother put her two cents in our relationship and told both of us "Clinton needs to run the fuck away from you as fast as hell!"

Ever since she said that, my feelings changed drastically. My feelings were already changed but mentally, I knew it was a matter of time before our relationship ended. April 13, I left to go out on the town with my Bestie Timothy for his Family Reunion in Baltimore. I drove the four hours to Timothy in North Carolina, then we took Timothy's car to Baltimore. This would be the first time other than Clinton going to Vegas that we took separate trips. It felt great not having to be overshadowed by Mister!

We both called and texted throughout the weekend. I had so much fun with my second family. Everyone knew me without even having to be introduced. Everyone knew I was Timothy's Bestie. I spent most of the time at the Family Reunion holding Timothy's baby cousin. She was 10 months and loved me and I loved her. On my way back home, I called Clinton to let him know how close I was. I told him that I needed some "Special attention!"

By the time I got home, Clinton was sleep on the couch. No food cooked, house was a mess and I felt different after getting "ready!" I got drunk, beat my meat and went to sleep. Clinton finally started a new job the week of April 18. I had to take him back and forth because he didn't have a car and I was not doing the rental thing again. His schedule worked great with my school schedule so I took him back and forth for the first couple of days.

A couple of days on the job, Clinton had him a "New friend!" He texted me Thursday April 20, and said he was invited to a smoke party and he'd be home shortly after. No biggie, enjoy yourself I thought but I replied, "OK!" The next day I text after he got off work and asked if he need me to come and get him, he said to meet him at Kroger's by the old house. HHMMMM OK.

By Sunday, he and his new friend were Best friends. I hadn't met this new guy, nor had I been invited to chill even though I didn't smoke anymore. Hell, he knew my entire circle and had a problem if he didn't. But I didn't have a problem, nor did I show I did. I kept it cute! The next week, same thing: His co-worker was going to bring him home so I didn't need to pick him. That night April 27th, I had cooked dinner and was "ready" because we hadn't had sex since the beginning of April.

Clinton didn't come home until 1 a.m. and was drunker than a skunk and passed out on the couch snoring. Now I had already been through this shit with Paul and I knew the signs. *Your ass just had sex!* is what I was thinking. *I may have been born at night, but it definitely wasn't last night, stupid!* I put the food up, walked the dogs, got drunk, beat my meat and passed out.

Saturday afternoon, Clinton left and text me later that night saying, "I'll be home shortly, downtown walking around!"

Get yo life nicca but I just texted back "OK!" That was the only thing I was saying going forward in my head to the fuckery he was doing, "OK!"

By now it was May 1st, and I was over his ass! I was far from stupid, yet he was watering grass on the other side thinking this grass was brown, so he could have stayed over there and kept watering that grass because now our grass was dead. I had a mental funeral and Clinton was dead to me, we were just roommates. We were not having sex, we couldn't have a conversation, he wasn't doing what he was supposed to do here at this house so someone else house was getting what this house needed and I was fine with that!

Diane and I went shopping on May 3rd to get our graduation outfits. Her ass made me try on everything I looked at. I was irritated but I felt her. She picked out some sharp shit for me. I wanted to wear pink and black so I got a fitted pink dress shirt from Express, some black slacks from Ross and she brought me some pretty ass socks with pink in them. I loved my school sister!

Clinton sent Diane a message on Facebook while we were eating so I called him. He said he needed her phone number because his friend had a job for her. His ass was lying! He just wanted to make sure I was out with Diane, being that I had not been out doing whatever the fuck he was. I wasn't dirty like him so I didn't do the shit he did to try and see what was going on!

I called Miyasha to tell her about what Clinton had just done. She started laughing and I'm like, "Bitch why you are laughing so hard?!"

Miyasha said, "Clinton was texting her last week when I was with her asking about how her kids were doing!"

I'm like bitch stop lying because when I got home he was snoring, sound asleep! Funny because Miyasha stayed a couple blocks from us but she said they were still texting after I called her and told her I was at home about to cook! **Twilight Zone Music**

Timothy had arrived on the evening of May 4th. My sister and her Bestie arrived a little after him and TaQuan was in the air on the way. Timothy came straight to our house and I was getting ready to go to the barbershop. I was dying my hair in the bathroom when Timothy rang the doorbell. I let him in and went back to the bathroom dying my hair. Timothy followed behind and we had small talk before Clinton came in the house rushing up the stairs like something was wrong.

Clinton came in the bathroom as if he didn't know whose car that was outside in the driveway. Timothy spoke to him and he gave him a dry ass hello. Timothy went down stairs because he knew if he didn't Clinton would be running up and down the steps and making a lot of noise and I finished up dying my goatee and hair.

After I was done, I went downstairs and let Timothy know I was ready to go. Clinton asked, "Where you about to go?"

I said, "To go get a haircut then meet my sister at the hotel."

Clinton said, "You didn't think I needed a haircut?"

I said, "Well, you've been out all day and you didn't think you needed a haircut?"

Clinton said, "I was dealing with my car trying to make sure I get this check for it."

I said, "OK," and left. *Fuck him!*

I got my haircut, picked up TaQuan from the airport and we headed to meet my sister. Clinton texted me and asked, "Guess I'll meet your sister at the graduation tomorrow?!"

I replied, "Yep!" I didn't give a shit whether he met her or not! I didn't give a shit about him! *Fuck him and his mother!* I was pissed!

Timothy, TaQuan and myself hung out with my sister and her Bestie until later that night. We had a ball talking in depth about my ending relationship and why I wasn't fighting for it like I fought for the relationship with Paul. Afterwards, I dropped TaQuan off at his friends because he didn't feel comfortable staying with me, then Timothy and I headed back to my place.

Clinton was awake when I got home. He said nothing to me and at first and I said nothing to him. After I got everything together for the next morning, I took him a graduation ticket downstairs and told him "he would have to ride with Timothy, TaQuan and Miyasha to the graduation because I had to be there extra early for rehearsal." I went back upstairs and he followed behind me.

Here his ass was trying to start an argument! I wasn't even having it and told him flat out, "Look nicca, I graduate tomorrow. My friends and family are here from out of town and this is my time! Keep all that negative shit to yourself because I don't have the time nor energy for it!" Just to think, I turned down a Branch Manager position at a Bank in Minnesota because he didn't want to move there because Paul was living in Minnesota. I really didn't want to move there either but it was a job paying good money!

******

May 5th, I graduated with my mother fucking Bachelor's Degree! I just didn't graduate, my ass graduated Cum Laude on the **Kappa Beta Delta Honor Society!** I DID THAT! WITH TEARS IN MY EYES, I DID THAT!

Clinton was with me the entire time of those two years for school and he didn't show up at my graduation! While sitting with my class and seeing my family from both my mom and dad's side and my friends, I didn't see my man! Talking about hurt! I was crying so hard and everyone thought I was crying because I was graduating. I was crying because Clinton wasn't there to witness my accomplishment! I knew I was single after receiving my Degree! On to better things because one monkey wasn't going to stop my show!

After graduation, everyone went to Red Lobster. My sister was asking where Clinton was. I said I didn't know. Miyasha then said, "I don't want to spoil the mood but I know why he didn't show up!"

Everyone was asking her why! She didn't say anything at first until I told her to say something being she already brought it up! She said, "Clinton called me this morning and told me that you and Timothy had been secretly fucking for years and he wasn't riding with Timothy at all!"

"GET THE FUCK OUT OF HERE!" That's exactly what I said—GET THE FUCK OUT OF HERE! "Everyone that knows us knows that Timothy is my best friend! There has never been anything sexual between us! We aren't even attracted to each other. We are not lesbians because that's what would have happened if we ever did anything! We both like the same thing so that would never be!"

This nicca was reaching for the sky to find out who I was fucking. He was missing every angle he hit because I wasn't fucking anybody, including him! We continued our dinner and decided to meet later back at my house to pre-game before the club. When we returned to the house, Clinton wasn't there. Thank GOD! I didn't need to see him at that time! I probably would have said something negative and ruined my moment!

However, once everyone was there by 11pm, Clinton came through the front door! Interesting because he never uses that door! He spoke to my sister, her best friend and my cousin Antoinette. He didn't speak to any of my male friends, nor did he say anything to me. I was cool with that because by this time, everyone including myself knew the real Clinton.

We all left, my sister and her bestie went back to the hotel and we all went to Bulldogs to party! I was about to have a blast because these last two years had been the hardest, educational wise, in my life. I was ready to release the stress of school and celebrate the fact that I was now single!

It's crazy how the universe works because it was right about this time when I received a message from an old fling on messenger. Derek was someone I had hooked up with years ago. He was 5'8", maybe 155 pounds, chocolate, a nurse, in the Navy from Virginia, with pretty ass feet and he'd recently moved back to Atlanta.

Derek saw my graduation picture on Facebook and wanted to congratulate me. I was all smiles when I read his message. I gave him my number and told him to call me. Derek called immediately and we talked halfway to the club before Timothy told me to hang up so we could sing our favorite song by Beyoncé, "Scared of Lonely!" I was anything but scared of lonely, however the song was my shit. I would rather struggle alone than have a motherfucker bringing me down. I'd been there and done that with Paul and here it was happening again. I needed out ASA mother-fucking P!

When we walked in the club, I felt like a free woman! LITERALLY! I was single like a dollar bill and I was ready for whatever the night had to offer! I got my free drinks from my friends and cousin and hit the dance floor. I was lit and getting my entire life! I just graduated with a Bachelor's Degree!

This was the third time I had been to a club without Mister! Whenever Clinton and I went to the club together, everyone thought he was my security guard or knew he was my boyfriend. He would hoover over me. If I got bumped accidentally, he was ready to fight. He never smiled or danced in the club. His whole vibe was terrifying in the club after we started dating.

He would be sure to hold me from the back, kiss me, or make others uncomfortable if they even looked at me. I understood the fact that we were lovers and wanting to show affection, but not every time, damn. I just wanted to have fun and be free.

******

By Monday, after everyone left, it was back to the real world. I was looking for a job and looking for a place to move. I hadn't uttered a consonant, vowel, syllable nor sent a smoke signal to Clinton since May 4th. I had absolutely nothing to say and I wanted to keep it just like that while living under the same roof as him.

I ended up calling the police again because he was trying to argue. Every day he was either making the alarm go off, slamming the doors, marching up and down the stairs, having his phone on speaker talking about me or bursting into the room because I had the door shut at first. I was sick of the alarm going off every time he opened the door, so I called Xfinity and told them to come get their shit! It wasn't like the bill was being paid anyway.

A guy from Xfinity ended up coming out Wednesday May 10th early in the morning. Clinton was gone so it wasn't a problem to unhook that shit and give him everything. Clinton returned home just a little after midnight. I was in the shower and I heard someone trying to get into the bathroom and beating on the door. I had locked the door because I didn't feel safe in the house with him. He was going off on the other side of the door.

Clinton yelled, "Don't be locking no fucking doors in my got damn house! Where the fuck is my screen for the security system?" I told him the guy from Xfinity took all the equipment! Clinton yelled, "My shit better be back here within an hour while beating on the door!" I didn't have time, so I just called the police. The police came out, took our statements, and told us to live in separate areas of the house.

Clinton said he wanted me out of his house because he paid the deposit. I said, "I just paid rent, I'm on the lease, but trust and believe I'll be gone by the first of the month!" The police left after giving us a card with the report information on it!

After that bull shit, I called the police officer Cam that came out the first time. I remember he said if I needed to talk or needed him, call. Cam picked up the phone and said, "Hello?"

I said, "Hey what's up guy? This is Samuel, the guy whose house you came to with the crazy ass boyfriend who was in my laptop posting shit on Facebook. I know it's late as hell but I needed someone to talk to."

Cam replied, "I know who you are! Where are you and are you safe?"

I promise I wanted to break down and cry, but I just said, "I'm good, just need someone to talk to."

Cam told me to meet him at "Friends," a bar in downtown Atlanta. It was already after 1am but I threw on some clothes, not even trying to look cute and punched it. Clinton was sitting on my couch talking to someone on speaker phone telling them I was about to leave and it was after 1am. Really bitch, when you've been in and out this mother fucker since the end of April and I didn't question yo ass not once!

I met Cam in the parking lot. He gave me a hug when I exited my car and I wanted to melt into his arms but I didn't. We went into the bar and he bought me a couple of drinks and a shot. We talked about everything under the sun and soon it was closing time. Time had just flown by. He told me I was spending the night at his place because he didn't want me to go home and run into a disturbance.

That's when I asked, "Are you gay bro?!" I didn't know if he was or not. I thought he was just being a cool friend.

Cam said, "Yes I am, you didn't realize you're in a gay-friendly bar?"

I told him, "Everything around me was cloudy and my mind was not here at all." I went home with Cam and spent the night.

That was the very first time I had had sex with anyone else since being with Clinton! But I was single now!

The next afternoon I went home and Clinton wasn't there, thank GOD! I called Cam after walking Brooklyn and Lacey and told him I was home and alone. We chatted for a few before he told me to get dressed so we could go somewhere. I asked where were we going, and Cam told me don't worry just get dressed! I put on my clothes and left out.

We ended up at one of his friend's house. We just hung out, he introduced me to everyone that came over. It was a Barbeque and friends playing spades. I felt good in the atmosphere, I had no worries. By the time I headed back home, it was after 2 a.m. I stopped at Kroger down the street from the house because I had used the last bit of toilet paper. Clinton hadn't bought any house supplies, let alone groceries since April after his grandmother sent him some money. However, he had weed every day, Reggie weed that is! **Laughing** I'm quite sure he had his coke too because he was always sniffing with nothing coming out, getting up extra early and not going to sleep. That was a habit I noticed in February when he got laid off.

When I got home from Kroger, I could hear Clinton coming through the garage. He had someone on speaker phone and he was snapping. Clinton was saying, "I just caught him cheating! He just dropped some dude off in a raggedy black car at Kroger! This bitch been cheating on me the whole time!"

I let his ignorant ass continue to talk without saying shit. He wanted a response or reaction from me, but I wasn't going to give him the time of day. That's when my sister called my phone. LaShenia said, "Are you stupid, why would you do that right by the house, you know he was following you right?!"

I told my sister, "This nicca is lying! Stop listening to him! I didn't drop anyone off! I just left from with my home boy Cam! Furthermore, if I'm going to fuck with anybody, I'm not dropping nobody off! Please believe they will have a car, crib and career!" I made sure to say that loud, so Clinton could hear me. Then I took my ass to sleep, happy! How are you going to be mad because I pulled a you on you? **Fuck You Mean Look**

That next morning, I decided I wasn't going to walk Brooklyn and Lacey any longer. It hurt my feelings to neglect them babies because they had absolutely nothing to do with this situation, but I wasn't going to be a babysitter either. Clinton came and went as he pleased and he knew my heart was with them babies.

Before long, they were shitting and pissing all downstairs everywhere. They were pissing on the rug, the wall and their beds. It was heart breaking but I lived upstairs. I didn't even eat nor cook in the kitchen anymore. I had been eating out since I graduated. Clinton cooked one time since I graduated but I didn't trust that shit. The downstairs of the house smelt just like shit, piss and Clinton's feet!

Clinton's feet were fucked up. I had only touched them thangs once and never again. They didn't stink — they stank! I loved him so I overlooked it. I would ask him to wash his feet daily. Especially on the days when he worked! He would come home, take his socks off and slide his feet across the carpet. I used to cringe when I seen that.

The day before I moved out on May 31st, I had to wash clothes at the Laundromat. Cam met me there and we talked the night away. I went back home, and Clinton wasn't there. Early the next morning, he began banging on the bedroom asking for his clothes hamper. He knew I had gone washing because I left the baskets downstairs in the living room and woke up and brought them into the bedroom I was staying in.

Clinton beat on the door instead of knocking and asked loudly, "Can I get my clothes hamper now please?!" He really didn't even need the hamper; the bastard just wanted it because I had it. I told him to give me a minute because I was unpacking the hamper and folding clothes. Not even five minutes had gone by and he began to beat on the door again asking for his clothes hamper. I just poured the clothes on the bed and gave him his shit because he was getting on my fucking nerves.

I only had one more day anyway to put up with this bullshit. Then the bastard had the nerve to ask, "What did I do to you to be so evil towards me" as I opened the door to hand him his shit! I paused for a moment as I looked him in the eyes and said "Really!" Then after that, I closed the door! What the fuck was I supposed to say to that when he already knew the answer?! I wasn't the one or the two, so I kept my fucking mouth shut! Not today motherfucker, not today!

The day of the move June 1st, Derek helped me because Cam had to work. Everyone knows I don't do manual labor because that shit hurt, but my ass was lifting shit like it was nothing. I surprised myself by lifting my couch and loveseat. They were the heaviest things I had to move. But Derek and I were in and out within two hours! I was the "Incredible Hulk" that day!

CHAPTER 5

Reaching Out

This man reached out to everyone I knew. When I say everyone, I mean everyone that he felt would take his side! He reached out to people from far away to close to me including my sister, Miyasha, Kevin, Dexter, George, Jermeal, David, Diane, Timothy, Cam and even my ex-husband Paul! WOW!! Speechless!!

I could expect and accept anyone Clinton reached out to except my ex-husband of all people! After a while, I wasn't even surprised being the way he acted the last month I lived in our home. Clinton was angry, hurt, and bitter, and he became an evil demon!

Clinton started reaching out to my sister right before she left to go back home to California. My sister let me know Clinton was sending her messages on Facebook and they had exchanged numbers. My sister remained neutral in the situation because she feared for my safety once she left Atlanta.

My sister had witnessed firsthand how my relationship with Paul almost turned deadly so she wanted to stay in contact with Clinton as much as possible. I assured her Clinton was nothing like Paul. I didn't know how far Clinton would go but I felt he was nothing like Paul. Clinton asked my sister questions she didn't have the answers to so she asked me for the answers.

I basically told LaShenia, after seeing my father as a cokehead while growing up I learned the signs, I see those same traits in Clinton. Clinton is very insecure and he doesn't take care of his responsibilities. He doesn't care if his bills are paid or not. "Clinton told me that he would pay bills when he could." He didn't even open his mail when it came, the unopened letters would sit there unless he felt it was important.

I told my sister, "I didn't want someone who has to depend on others to pay bills!" When times get tough, he ran to family. I didn't have that and I would have to tackle my tough times and I always got the job done. We were cut from different cloths when it came to that. Lastly, I just couldn't take his feet or his lack of cleanliness. I was confused on how he could clean houses when the tub in our main bathroom looked like it hadn't been cleaned in years!

Clinton reached out to Miyasha to ask her, "Had he ever made her feel uncomfortable?!"

She told him, "No." Miyasha was very neutral just like my other friends. None of my friends took a side unlike Clinton's mother even after he snapped out. However, Miyasha did feel that Clinton would only reach out to her just to ask questions or talk about me.

Clinton reached out to David, TaQuan's ex-boyfriend. Unfortunately, David told Clinton I was cheating on him. I was so confused on even why David would say anything of that nature about me. I'd known David for five years and our relationship was great to my understanding. We had never had any type of disagreement. We used to talk here and there sometimes.

I met David the same time I met TaQuan, Kevin, Moe after Timothy introduced us back in September of 2012. I took more to TaQuan as he became my mentor. I had never had a conversation with David about any other male while I was with Clinton so

I was caught off guard and flabbergasted by the accusations of me cheating.

David had sent a lot of long text messages to Clinton talking about TaQuan and me. Not us being together but just things about us. Clinton used David to get information, which was false information at that. Clinton took that information and ran with it, embellishing it whenever possible.

Clinton then contacted Diane and sent her everything that David sent him. He had been talking with Diane every chance he got about me. She was sick of it and the days we went to school she would always have something new that Clinton told her about me. Clinton had only met Diane once! However, Diane knew more lies about me than anyone else from Clinton. Diane sent me the text messages from Clinton that David sent him. I forwarded all the messages to TaQuan because after Clinton told me that David said I was cheating, I didn't believe it at first.

David denied everything until being confronted with the messages. David then apologized and said he was angry that's why he had said those things. Angry or not, Clinton believed them and there was no taking back what was said. I was angry with David but I let it go because I had known him for a long time. He didn't cause us to break up because that was already in the making.

Clinton was posting everything on Facebook about us, more so about me. Everyone was sending me screenshots of everything this dummy was talking about. I didn't bother to go reading them myself, I went to his page and, deleted and blocked him. I had no time for those mind games. He had fucked me enough!

Some people in my own circle shocked me the most. Well, in all honesty, I really wasn't shocked. I looked at it as a petty pay back for Kevin. Being that I met George, Dexter and Jermeal through Kevin, it was only right that they follow behind him. Clinton contacted Kevin and Kevin told Clinton anything deceitful about me as possible.

I would find out later that Kevin told Clinton about the club, about me looking at his phone on Jack'd and Tumbler and more so importantly, Kevin invited Clinton over to his new home to discuss me and about Dexter. Dexter had flirted with me multiple times. I never told Clinton. However, I told Kevin and George. George said Dexter flirted with him too! In fact, George said, "Dexter tried to fuck me too girl!" to Kevin and myself.

Kevin went back and told Dexter what I said, but apparently left out what George said. Go figure, he wouldn't spill the tea on his good girlfriend, but will spill the tea about me! No shade, I get it! This one tooth bitch, funk smelling breath, pregnant looking stomach, loud mouth bitch was still upset that I sucked her nephew's dick for a hot second!

Girl get over it, I did that a long time ago! He's mad because he doesn't really have a relationship with his nephew and when we spoke about his nephew I asked, "How is your nephew?"

And this jealous bitch said, "We haven't spoken in a minute!"

I said, "That's too bad, he hit me up recently!" I told that child her nephew was gay! **Blank Stare**

Any who, after these bitches met up over Kevin's to discuss their Queen (ME), Dexter was mad. I tagged Dexter, Kevin and a lot of other people on Facebook that I had ever taken a picture with that was in my phone. Dexter commented back under his picture and said, "Untag me, I don't want people thinking I like you!" I texted him back because I was confused.

Dexter said, "This picture makes it look like I like you, but I don't!"

I said, "No it doesn't bro!"

Dexter replied, "No, I mean as a friend G!"

I said, "Huh?"

Dexter said, "Man I know what you said about me trying to get wit Clinton and I ain't wit it."

I told Dexter, "I said Clinton told me you were trying to get with him! I didn't say you were trying to get with him!!"

Dexter then replied, "I was told you were showing texts to other people that me and Clinton had….but I don't even have that nigga's number. Never texted him."

I said, "Never happened!"

Well come to find out, I showed Kevin a text message that Clinton sent me stating, "Someone in my circle had been hitting on him in the messenger app." Clinton had cropped the message, so I didn't know who sent it. Clinton said it was between Dexter, Veno and Victor.

I never confronted any of them, I just told Kevin! Well after that I gained two enemies; Dexter and the boy Clinton is talking to best friend, someone I never met in my life. This dude started sending me messages on messenger about Clinton. I was so lost. Why is a nicca sending me messages that I never met off some shit Clinton said about me? This was a Paul situation all over again and I just cut off all their asses: Kevin, Dexter, George and Jermeal! Birds of a feather flock together and there is no room for drama this way niccas! Take that fag shit elsewhere!

It fucked with my mind as to why Clinton was reaching out to everyone I knew rather than sticking to his circle that barley came around us. But then I thought, "If my life is miserable with my friends, why not make Sam's life miserable with his friends!" Clinton's friends were rarely seen. He said his best friend Will liked him, so he didn't want to be around him, Jamella was busy with her life and Todd worked and traveled too much.

Unfortunately, that only left my friends for Clinton to be around. He ran off all my straight friends by looking at them funny. He assumed they were gay or messed around with me. My straight homies said, "They wouldn't come back around as long as Clinton was in the picture!" They made a promise to that and if I was with Clinton, I didn't hear from them!

Clinton has bumped into Cam twice since we'd broken up. Once at Wal-Mart and the other time was at Popeye's. Clinton told Cam, "He never had a fair chance with me, he knew where I lived, I cheated on him multiple times and one of the men drove a black car!" Cam was laughing inside because he didn't understand why Clinton was even telling him those things because he didn't care.

I was shocked at all the people Clinton reached out too but the most shocking one ever was my ex-husband! This deranged, insecure ass nicca actually reached out to my ex-husband Paul on Facebook! He told Paul everything that happened! I guess he thought Paul would side with him because Paul is my ex and I had written my books, *Eyes Without A Face, How It All Happened,* and *Why Did We Meet,* with him in it!

Wrong! My ex-husband wasn't going and after a few messages back and forth, asked Clinton to stop hitting him up! I know that must have been a slap in the face! That was the ultimate for me, and a deal closer. I already didn't want anything to do with Clinton. I may have spoken if I bumped into him in public, but after reaching out to Paul, Clinton was dead to me!

The crazy part about Clinton was, even after I moved out, we still shared my P.O. BOX. I checked it regularly, never stole his mail or took his name off the box. He had a key and I didn't want to ask for it back because I didn't want to talk to him. He had important mail coming in and I left that shit there! He should have picked up on my character then if he didn't know while being in a relationship with me.

******

Clinton told me many, many times, "You'll never meet another man like me!"

"My ex-husband Paul said the same thing! I always reply in return, first of all, Thank GOD!"

After I moved out, I received my first utility bill. Clinton had paid it with a Insufficient Funds check online, just to get my address. I was charged a $30 fee for the returned check! I called the company and found out Clinton paid $40 towards my "new bill" online! By paying my bill online in my new place, he got my address in return. What type of sick shit was he on?! Who the fuck does that?! I guess you can call me "Hoover!" Apparently, I just suck these ignorant, insecure fools, right on up!

CHAPTER 6

Loyalty Is Royalty

I'm going to keep this chapter short and to the point! There is no mending these friendships what-so-ever, so everything I say will stick like glue and I'm saying with my middle finger, "Fuck You!" This is exactly why I keep my grass cut low, so I can see the snakes. This is the primary reason why I don't have too many gay people in my circle too! Even the devil was once an angel!

Everyone that I'm writing about had just taken a trip together a year ago for Halloween. We all met down in New Orleans and partied for the weekend and got white boy wasted. We tried to do an intervention with Kevin because everyone in the circle was saying, "He's an alcoholic and an embarrassment when he's drunk!" The intervention didn't go so well!

We all know Kevin is an alcoholic! Intervention won't help him because his close friends tried, and it absolutely did nothing but make this fool drink more. Kevin drinks everyday that ends in y! He parties just about every day that ends in y. Some of us including his best friend George always ask, "What is this bitch celebrating?!" She's either late on her rent or car payment every month but you better believe she has money for the clubs and alcohol!

His ex-boyfriend told the circle a long time ago that Kevin is careless when it comes to money and paying bills. This is where Kevin and Clinton have the most in common! Kevin's best friend took Kevin's ex-boyfriend! While Kevin was busy running the streets, attending every party, being Atlanta's Elite, someone else was making sure his boyfriend was straight. I guess the alcohol was pretty strong because his ass didn't see his bestie sliding in for the kill on his man!

Kevin did a lot of questionable things with his life with his ex-boyfriend that I can guarantee he wishes he had done differently, that's one of the things we have in common! This dummy almost lost her job playing with FMLA, using it when she didn't need too. She would make sure not to post pictures and turn off her location whenever she called out! And despite the fact of having the greatest dental plan of all times through her employer, this dummy still had a rancid smell of rotting meat from her mouth that none of us will ever forget! Kevin always covered his mouth while laughing and smiling instead of fixing the problem. It's crazy because the one's that talk the most shit be the main one's that smile and never show their teeth!

The other thing Kevin and I had in common was being in an abusive relationship. I would never make fun or poke jokes about that because I know the depth of the situation and the scar that it leaves on you rather in or out of the relationship. Kevin and his ex-boyfriend seemed to be fighting all the time. However, the circle only knew about two fights. George informed us on the other two and Kevin ex's damaging his car. Kevin would have never told us this, but George had no problem telling. Our loyalty within the group remained sacred because we never told Kevin that we knew he got beat up two more times more than he told us.

George said one time Kevin actually started the fight with his ex-boyfriend while he was drunk. I wonder if it had something to do with Kevin stealing bottles of alcohol from parties he visited in Atlanta. Kevin would go to a party and steal bottles if they were laid out. In fact, one party we all went too, Kevin asked Clinton to look out as his ex-boyfriend tried to steal a couple of bottles from a party. However, he was caught and put out due to Kevin! **Shameless Look**

Jermeal only likes kids, well, guys that are too young for him. You know the ones that are 18 and under. He's about 24 or 25 and his motto is, "if he can pee, he's for me!" Jermeal was cool at first but I put nothing past him because of how he speaks about others in the group when they're not around. We all do that, but he never confesses to what he says if the subject is brought up.

George is a shit starter! He has always been the type to throw a rock and hide his hand! I could never trust this bitch and that's why I never told her anything that could come back and bite me in the ass! She's said many things about Kevin. That's how the circle knew that Kevin got beat up multiple times by his ex-boyfriend!

Dexter wants to fight me because of what Clinton and Kevin said but never asked me if I really said it! How sway! But it's not like he doesn't cheat on his fiancé from time to time! **Just Staring** with his painted hairline and his girlfriend with the high pitch voice!

Let me not forget Victor! Clinton would always ask if Victor was going out whenever we went out because he said, "Victor was more masculine than anyone in my circle!" I beg to differ, but it is what is.

Victor came onto me multiple times knowing I was with Clinton! He didn't care at all! Victor was probably the one who sent Clinton the message, but who knows. These hoes were hoes so who knows who sent the message to Clinton. Either way, I didn't care! Have at it because if a man is going to cheat, he's going to cheat regardless!

Victor was a thirsty dude from what Kevin said! Victor was going to pay to play or whatever it took to get his rocks off! Victor came at me multiple times, but I never said anything! I took him for what he is. A hoe!

Sometimes I feel that I should have whipped Kevin and George's asses when I had the chance! I wrote about that story in my second book, "How It All Happened!" But what good is fighting when your opponent can't fight! People who hate you are always looking for other people that hate you. Sometimes they go and recruit people too because they need hater help.

You only have one time to cross me and some of you within this chapter had two. Shame on me, not you! I learned it was never my enemies I had to watch out for, it was the ones screaming "I love you."

CHAPTER 7

Love Still Wins

When you thought that something was designed to set you back, it might just be what makes you stronger! I learned 7 years ago after the break up with my ex-husband that when you try to publicly humiliate someone you once loved, whose character does that speak to more; yours or theirs? I just must Thank GOD for my personal growth and keep moving forward no matter what. I refuse to claim ANYTHING negative over my life! My ex-boyfriend is a good man; he just wasn't good for me. But in the end, LOVE STILL WINS!

My past may be dark and dirty as hell, but my present is bright as the light and squeaky clean! Thank You GOD! All my situations changed when I met "Cam!" I knew whoever would be that special person; I was going to choose them wisely. It wouldn't be because they looked good to me physically, it was going to be because they felt good to me spiritually.

I wanted a spiritual connection. I wanted someone I would connect with and connect with over and over again. I wanted this person to stimulate my mind as well as body. That person ended up being Cam. Once again, I lost weight in my last relationship and gained it all back, plus some while being with Cam, he sure does look good on me.

Every time we made love it was brand new. Making love wasn't just having sex with Cam. I felt something other than "him!" Cam makes me feel like I have never been touched, like I didn't have any flaws. I love the explosive feelings I feel while he's inside of me. It's a feeling when I thought I was in love with someone, I actually wasn't.

I loved certain ways about them which made me feel they were the one. I knew Cam was the one because I felt every feeling that I longed for; security, warmth, welcomed, appreciated, admired, and most importantly, loved." Cam made me feel loved more than I felt I should be loved.

I knew Cam was the one because I wasn't worried about what he was doing out of my presence. I knew Cam was the one because I pictured our future and us being married. He kept my mind stimulated, heart going, and my body aroused even when I'm upset with him. More importantly, Cam never stopped looking at me like he did the very first time we met. I never felt like it was just sex with Cam.

I asked Cam, after a couple times of us making love, "how he felt about it" and he stated, "My sex life is amazing. The best I've had in a long time. There is never a dull moment. Its pleasure, I just can't get enough of it. It's like that roller coaster at the theme park that you want to get on over and over again. Anytime and anyplace! I like to be spontaneous, and to find someone that's on the same page is awesome."

I don't do the roller coaster rides at the theme park, but I knew what he was talking about. I love Cam. I never thought I would love someone more than Paul or #26. As I stated before, everything wasn't bad with Paul and nothing was wrong with #26, they were just not for me.

******

How do you want to build when you don't care what collapses? So, I had to teach myself to not get sidetracked by people who are not on track. As a person who's been through more than the average person can handle, I have no problem letting go of anything that causes me stress.

One thing for sure and two things for certain, I don't mind being talked about, just don't leave out the good stuff and give the respect of telling people the truth as I am doing right now. I knew I'd matured when I realized every situation didn't need a reaction. Sometimes you must leave people to do the ignorant shit they do!

I had to tell Derek I was sleeping with Cam and I told Cam I was sleeping with Derek. However, they knew each other already so it was cool. I decided that we should all sleep together. **Yes, I Sure Did, Stare** We all agreed, and we picked a day that everyone would be available to spend the night at Derek's place.

After I moved into my new place, the three of us spent the night at Derek's in the middle of June. I was happier than a kid in a candy store. Here it was, I had not one, but two beautiful men. It was like a straight man's fantasy; to have two beautiful women. I was about to get my life and I was more than ready. I had experienced this with my ex-husband Paul, but I wasn't ready then, well, I was ready now!

Derek had the place set up romantically with candles lit, some soft music on and dim lighting. Derek poured us all a drink while each of us sat on the king size bed. After a couple of drinks, we all started undressing and kissing each other. Thinking back on this has chills over my body right now! Derek was in front of me and Cam was behind me and we were all kissing each other before they traded places.

Once Cam got in front of me I was ready! Before I knew it, they both had made love to me and we all fell asleep. The next morning when we woke up, I felt like that was natural and that I had two boyfriends. I wanted them both and being that they were both verse, I figured we could all please each other. Hell, now, I felt verse too **Laughing Hysterically Out Loud** because generally I'm a bottom.

However, I had a sexual connection with both and I was ready for a whole entirely different level in life. A couple of days later, I decided I didn't want a 3-way relationship and choose Cam over Derek. There wasn't anything wrong with Derek; it was the fact that Derek was too busy. He worked long hours and was never available. I wanted consistency and Cam and I had a deeper relationship although I had known Derek first.

Derek understood, and Cam and I started dating each other. By now, we had been seeing each other for five months October and we decided we were ready for a relationship. Really, I decided I was ready for a relationship because Cam knew he wanted it since the first day we meet. I didn't want to do that right away because I still had the last relationship on my mind and I didn't want to be comparing him when shit went wrong.

So many of us jump in and out of relationships and it's because we don't want to be alone but in return, we don't have time to heal. You must be alone first before getting into a new relationship. Most people think that the best way to get over a relationship is to get under someone new. Well unfortunately, that's not true! When you do that, you bring the bitterness, unhappy thoughts with you and that new relationship becomes toxic.

I had gone to the doctor to do my regular blood work and test for any STDs on March 24th, and I weighed in at 161 pounds. Although I was in a relationship, my partner was accusing me of cheating and I know from rule of thumb, "that meant, possibly, my partner was cheating." I went back to the doctor May 8th, to be retested because I had only had sex with Clinton from that time and I weighed in at to 151. I had lost weight due to stress about my situation, not eating healthy and drinking excessively.

I believe my weight at 161 was primary alcohol. However, I went back to the doctor November 3rd, and I weighed in at 162 and no STDs! I was eating healthy home cooked meals and I wasn't drinking as much because I had nothing to stress about. In addition, my T-Cell count went back up as well. **I've Never Fallen below 200** ** In that case if your T-Cell falls below 200, you are diagnosed with AIDS instead of having HIV**

******

Clinton told me I needed him because I couldn't afford to live without him.

Financially, I'm back to where I was before I met Clinton. My bills are paid, credit cards paid off except one, I have a brand-new car, my credit score is above 700 and I have more money in the bank than I had before I met Clinton. BUT GOD! I promised myself after that relationship, "I would never go broke again another day in my life!"

My life is once again getting back on track and I'm farther ahead compared to where I was and the setbacks I'd experienced with Clinton. The saying is true, "You may have a hundred pennies, but four quarters is rare." My circle was reduced by the fake people that Clinton managed to manipulate and I'm grateful for it because it showed their true colors. I had those friends who loved me and remain by my side. In addition, Onsemious and the rest of the straight crew finally came back around soon as I moved into my own place.

Truth be told, and to be fair, I never get shit on twice! Play with a game, don't play with me. I play chess, not checkers, now check mate and check that. It's all fun and games until the rabbit has the gun. And when you think it's a game, I'll show you how the game is done.

I've learned to never shit on someone who made sure you were straight while they were struggling. I'm a very humble person. I don't have a bounce back game; I just have love in my heart! I'm confused at why someone would be consistently coming for me when I don't even know them.

I pray that my ex isn't doing what Paul did because that would be messed up on so many levels. Why am I being a topic of conversations? At the end of the day, we both needed peace and happiness. I'm not mad at all what that man has or is, doing right now! We must learn how to move forward and let go. We are too old for drama. Steve Harvey said men don't argue on Facebook when it comes to relationship issues.... He lied! My ex Clinton showed me that!

I promise you, I wish my ex nothing but the best. I have no ill will against him and I pray he gets everything he desires. I don't speak about him badly at all. In fact I don't even speak of him.

At the end of this relationship everything was based off assumptions. I guess with these messages I've received, I could assume my ex was already in a relationship before we were over and projected that energy on me because he was doing everything he accused me of.

Some people break-up mentally long before they breakup physically and a person can think they have the other on "LOCK" while lying beside them all the while the other person's mind is in another place. Be careful how you treat people because once you lose their head, the body follows.

Always keep a piece of you for you. That's not selfish, that's survival. There are two sides to every story, and then there are my screenshots. Sometimes the betrayal is the blessing. You take the real "L" when you play somebody who never had any intentions on playing you. If you're not doing better than the person you're talking about, maybe you shouldn't be talking about them.

If you're wishing for my downfall, you can forget it. GOD didn't bring me this far to leave me. Now I don't know who you serve, but I serve a mighty, mighty GOD. AMEN! You owe yourself the love that you so freely give to other people. I am living proof that MY GOD can do anything!

I always tell people, "stop leaving out the part of the story where you fucked up!" Replacing me is easy, but getting them to give you the same feeling I do is impossible. Have you ever stopped fucking with somebody and nothing, but good shit been happening ever since? **Raises Hand** If someone is doing better ever since they left you, then maybe you really were the problem.

It's crazy that I learned the guilty dog barks the loudest; the guilty cat rarely makes a sound. I have to say this in the humblest way possible, "I didn't lose you. You lost me. You'll search for me in everyone you're with and I won't be found!"

I learned many things and I can compile them in this message; I would rather struggle and work hard for everything I have then have someone tell me, "You wouldn't have that if it wasn't for me!" My setback was a blessing! I survived what was meant to destroy me. I came back like a boss…fabulous, wiser and stronger than ever.

While you're praying on my downfall, I'm praying you get on your footing, that's how I know we're definitely not the same! Sometimes silence is the best answer because it can never be misquoted. I will always associate myself with people of excellent quality, for it's better to be alone than in bad company. Nobody can make you happy until you're happy with yourself first.

Lastly, to hold a grudge means you've decided to have a permanent seat at the misery table. I don't care what "Benefits" you bring to the table. If your energy is bad for my mental health, you cannot eat with me! If I don't know anything else, I know that "Love Still Wins," even if I'm single!

When someone loses respect and no longer wants to argue with you, it's a wrap. I've slept on a bed, slept on the floor, slept on the couch, but I never slept on myself and I will never be ashamed of my struggle!

Some quotes I used, the authors are unknown.

Clinton is an ALLEGED COKE HEAD

To Whom It May Concern:

No relationship is ever a waste of time! If it didn't bring you what you want, it taught you what you didn't want! Stop being bitter!

When you are actually POWERFUL, you don't need to be petty!

While you were busy with him, I met him. While you were with him, I ran to him. When you didn't call, I called him. When you weren't there, he was.

By the way, he says, "Thank You!"

LOVE WILL ALWAYS WIN!

www.ingramcontent.com/pod-product-compliance
Lightning Source LLC
Chambersburg PA
CBHW062103290426
44110CB00022B/2697